HAPPINESS NOW

Appreciation
Makes it Happen

Frances B. Lancaster

*Dear Melody,
Love,
Grandma L*

W

WISEWOMAN PRESS

Happiness Now: Appreciation Makes it Happen

Edited by Ruth L. Miller
Managing Editor: Michael Terranova

ISBN: 978-0-945385-87-5

WiseWoman Press,
Vancouver, Washington 98665

www.wisewomanpress.com
pra4all@comcast.net

Printed in U.S.A.

Lovingly dedicated
in deep appreciation to my deceased husband, John,
who kept our home fires burning, turned our
yard into a garden sanctuary,
and faithfully gave his life
to serving his family
as husband, dad and grandpa.

Table of Contents

FOREWORD

Happiness is someone to love, something to do, and something to look forward to.
Author unknown

To live in the state of appreciation is one of life's greatest gifts. People who live in this manner emanate a feeling of peace. They seem to enjoy life and are fun to be around. They are awake to the blessings of the creative spirit within themselves. They share from their abundance and benefit from the great law of circulation that multiplies their gifts; therefore, their abundance grows in a systematic manner. They have learned to trust the Infinite for their supply and celebrate with a grateful heart. The following stories show how appreciation benefited two families in entirely different ways.

Ward and Alma were the happiest people I have ever had the pleasure of knowing. They were almost retired by the time I met them, and their lives revealed a generous amount of kindness and wisdom. They embodied each of the key aspects that you will find in the following chapters of Happiness Now. They understood appreciation of self, others, abundance, beauty, order, wisdom, creativity, holiness and prayer. They exhibited confidence within themselves and were a joy to be around; their eyes sparkled, and their interest in the happenings of your life, made you feel valuable and cherished. You could feel the strong connection between their souls as they laughed and smiled at each other.

From the time Ward and Alma were married, they lived on the same piece of land that was given to them for a wedding gift. Over the sixty or more years of their marriage, their tiny house grew in size as the years passed. A room was added here; another there, a garage was added and modified, all reflecting the inner expansion of their awareness of their Spiritual identity. They understood

iii

their Oneness with their Creator and the gifts that have been bestowed upon all of us, if we will but pause and appreciate where we are. They deeply appreciated life, each other, and the many people who were drawn into their circle of love and happiness.

My, how they demonstrated abundance! It just came naturally as they cared for and appreciated the wonderful things that came into their lives through gifts, inheritance or plain hard work. Alma collected dolls, 100 of them. They all had names, beautiful clothes, and their unique story. Ward even closed in his carport to make a special room for Alma to display her precious treasures as her collection grew. That's not all. Alma inherited her mother's sterling silver eating utensils as well as Ward's family silverware. There were felt-lined boxes of sterling silver stacked along one whole wall in their spare room. She would tell how she had created pieces of silverware by just thinking of them. Soon she was led to a person or place where she could purchase the missing piece even if these items were rare and hard to find. Much happiness was shared as she told stories about the collections filling the rooms of their home.

Their three acres were filled with floral beauty in the summer time. Alma collected rare, old fashioned roses and took great delight in planting a hydrangea garden where she nurtured the soil in a way to produce deep purple flowers from each plant. A walk around their garden was an adventure in the restoration of one's soul.

It took three hours to mow the grass on their grounds, but Ward would ride his mower and make the trip at least once a week as the season progressed, because order and beauty go together. There was a little garden house on the back side of the property where they kept the tools and other equipment for outdoor maintenance. In one corner was a table with two chairs neatly placed for respite from the sun or work as they paused for a drink of coffee or lemonade. Order included balance and harmony in all things for these two happy people.

Ward was an electronics buff although he wasn't adept with computers, because they hadn't come into common use during his life. His hobby was recording spiritual messages on cassette tapes, and then he would give them to anyone who would take time to listen. It was such a joy to watch him share the wisdom he was acquiring through the inspiring speakers he had recorded. He gave over 250 tapes to one eager student, myself, and literally changed my life with the new ideas these tapes presented.

Alma's inquisitive and thirsty mind, however, was drawn to the library to study the ancient writings of spiritual teachers written in other languages. During one winter vacation in Hawaii, she translated some of these from Greek to English just for the fun of it. Her efforts brought great joy, and her eyes simply gleamed as she told you about it. Their love of spiritual truth happily sent them to three different churches on Sunday mornings while visiting the islands. They were opened-minded and appreciated hearing the different interpretations of topics that were dear to their hearts.

Their creativity was expressed through conversation while sitting around their big oak dining table, too. Alma would make a pot of tea using her lovely silver tea service and begin the dialog with a thought provoking question. Soon we were discussing ideas unaware of the time that was passing by. In the background were recording devices that Ward used to edit video tapes he had made from TV programs. He watched the movies again and removed the commercials. There were dozens of these tapes. His creative spirit never was long at rest without something to do.

Alma and Ward had such a connection to Spirit, to their own holiness, although they would not have called it that. Their lives simply spoke louder than words. One of the things I remember Alma sharing was a Spiritual Practice she engaged in before going to sleep at night. She said to me, "Now Honey, I hold up each of my ten fingers, one at a time, and count 10 different things for which I am grateful." I never forgot what she told me, and I know that just this one little practice can set the tone for good things to come the next day as well as assure a peaceful rest.

We didn't talk much about prayer, but some people's lives simply demonstrate their Spiritual connection as a walking, living prayer. Ward and Alma did this, and I am convinced that their happiness was the true test of their appreciation for the life they had created together and shared so generously with those around them. "Come, let us sit awhile on our beautiful garden bench," Alma would say. Together we rested in the coolness of the shade enjoying each other's company. They had mastered feeling, "Happiness Now!"

Happiness is being inspired by Spirit and watching your dream become your reality.

The photos you find in this book were taken by my grandmother between 1911 and 1918. My grandmother, Matilda Dorothy Benjamin Stringer Binder, and her bridegroom, William Henry Binder had a dream to own land. They arranged to homestead 160 acres near San Luis Obispo, California. At 41 years of age, she had acquired many skills, one of which was taking and developing her own photos. I am grateful to have such a detailed documentation of the progress of their homestead, lovingly named, Oak Terrace.

Matilda was blessed with a hardy, courageous, adventuresome spirit. She was orphaned at 9 years of age, married at 16, moved to California from Indiana with her baker husband, Fred, and had two children, one of whom died as an infant. During the Gold Rush of 1898, Matilda, Fred and 7 year old Clyde took a steam ship headed for Alaska, hoping to strike it rich. They couldn't find a claim, so they ran a restaurant in Dyea, Alaska, at the foot of the Chilcoot Trail where hundreds of souls trudged the steep mountainside on their way to the gold fields.

In 1899, the Gold Rush was mostly over. The little family eventually found its way back to California and passed through the beautiful area of San Luis Obispo near the Pacific Ocean. Back in Los Angeles a few years later, however, Matilda's husband was struck by a street car and died. She opened a dry goods store with the insurance settlement, and that's where she met my grandfather.

Her memory of the land through which she had traveled earlier was still burning in her heart. Here is where the dream began to germinate. That land could be theirs if they would develop it for seven years. Her young husband was happy to leave behind the memories of his childhood working in a coal mine in Kentucky. They labored together to fulfill their dream and created heaven on earth on their parcel of land. My father was born on the homestead a year later, and you will see how the family and their land evolved as the book progresses.

The photos are demonstrations of two people who truly appreciated the opportunity to create a new life. The work was hard, but the rewards were too numerous to count. You can feel their oneness with the Creator in the various ways they created beauty, order and holiness by the respect and union they felt with the land and its animals. In seven years, they tamed a wild and rugged countryside, turning it into an enchanted forest where people came from miles around to partake in a Sunday dinner.

There was always a sense of peace about my grandmother. I think it was because in her heart, she never ceased to appreciate her surroundings and add her own personal touch of beauty to them. The desire to create beauty in one's life is a direct reflection of our feelings of Oneness with our Creator. Peace and inner happiness are the natural result. I hope the photos will awaken your own desire to follow your dreams and create happiness for yourself and your loved ones here on earth.

May the ideas in the chapters, ideas that Ward and Alma lived by, as well as my grandparents, inspire you to smile often, enjoy deeper peace, and find lasting happiness in your own life. **Happiness Now** is always a choice. Through **Appreciation,** we reawaken the awareness of our inner connection to our Creator and return our hearts to their natural state of well being.

May God bless you on your journey to Happiness Now.

Child of God, you were created to create the holy,
the good and the beautiful.
God's will for you is perfect happiness.
A Course in Miracles

SPECIAL GRATITUDE

I would like to express my gratitude to Anne McKenrick for her thoughtful editing of my original manuscript. As a writer of many short stories and published works, I truly appreciate her willingness to work with me as I wove my way through the many ideas in this book.

Besides the listening ear of my husband John, I also had the help of Diane Allen and Sherry Franklin in editing my revision. An unexpected phone call from a long lost relative, Elizabeth Ballard, inspired me to get out my father's unpublished book, The Greatest Legacy. As I revisited his writings, I came to realize that many of the photos in it would be perfect for Happiness Now.

Thirdly, I want to express my gratitude to Ruth Miller for her joyful cooperation and encouragement in bringing forth this creative endeavor. My prayer partners, Patricia Taylor, Michael Terranova and June Moriyasu have been great supporters through all of my creative efforts. To my late mother, Ruth White Brown, I give credit for introducing me to metaphysical teachings which emphasize the connection between our thoughts and our experiences. I acknowledge my deceased father, Morton Binder, for the many ways he turned lemons into lemonade and danced to the music inside by creating beauty wherever he went. Thank you one and all.

With much love,

Frances

Chapter One

What It Means to Be Happy

Happiness is the meaning and the purpose of life,
the whole aim and end of human existence.
Aristotle

If you are reading this book, you have felt the contrast between being satisfied with life and yearning for more happiness. You have wondered why others seem to be filled with joy much of the time. What is it that makes some people move through difficult situations with a minimum of disruption? Why do others linger in the story of their misfortune for years after an incident has occurred? Why does tragedy follow a chosen few and leave their brothers and sisters seemingly untouched? Most important, is there really any way to find lasting happiness in my own life?

What does real happiness look like? Underneath all the definitions that come from our thoughts about what it is, lies the feeling of satisfaction. Being personal and coming from our feeling of connection with life, means that each person will arrive at his own criteria for being happy.

There are those who seem to draw a sense of happiness from acquiring things in the world of material objects or achievement through personal effort. Does this really work? It may temporarily give a sense of pleasure, but the deepest meaning of happiness goes far beyond having possessions or success as the world defines it. True happiness encompasses a greater view of life itself. When we see ourselves as an integral part of everything, and that we make a difference by what we contribute, we begin to have a greater sense of belonging. We feel our

1

oneness. We have begun to touch the Source of our true happiness. For as we see and feel our connection to others, we find ourselves expressing more of the love, joy, beauty, wisdom, and peace that is our true nature. It is by expressing our true nature that we come to discover real happiness.

Real happiness is a gift to humanity from our Source. It comes from within us, does not depend on outside circumstance, will not disappear when the stock market hits a slump or our partner leaves us. Since the Source is always present, being part of our inheritance, we can live in faith that our good will continue to flow to us. There will be other channels that open up. New opportunities will bring even greater experiences of satisfaction and pleasure. It is as though we possess the "magic lamp" of happiness right where we are. For it to become a reality, however, we may have to release our old ideas about how things should be. We may need to change our actions, because our unskilled behaviors can cloud out the sunshine that lives within us. Are we willing to change? Where do we begin? Do we have a plan? Do we really want to live in the awareness of true happiness?

In 1911, Matilda and William set out to
accomplish a dream. One hundred
sixty acres had to be tamed over the
next seven years for this land to be theirs.
Living in a tent for a year, they began their
labor of love building a chicken coop
followed by a house.

William starts constructing the foundation for the house.

After a year of work on the homestead,
this is how far along the house had come.
The fireplace would be a big job.

Baby Morton was also
born that first year to
forty-year-old Matilda
and a younger William.

Chapter 2

Beginning Where We Are

Every day is a fresh beginning, every morn is the world made new.
Sarah Chauncey Woolsey

There is a temptation to remember the past and its mistakes. Our first step in finding true happiness is to find a way to bring acceptance into our awareness. We can reframe our perception of what has happened up to now. Had we been gifted with greater insight, we no doubt would have reacted differently. We would have formed different beliefs about life. We could have realized that people or situations in our lives were there as opportunities to grow deeper in our awareness of oneness. Unskilled behaviors would have been accepted as just that. We would have been able to realize that negative actions and words were telling a story of belief in separation. We would have listened to our feelings as gages of truth or illusion. We would have considered feelings associated with love as being true and feelings of fear being indications of judgment, doubt and negativity, witnesses to the idea that we are separated from one another.

In order to create a new framework for establishing happiness as a way of life, we must be willing to examine our relationship with our Source, our Creator. Deep within us is everything beautiful, holy and wise. At some point in our lives, we have all felt this truth. Seeing our newborn child for the first time, watching the sunlight dancing on a mountain stream, feeling the exhilaration of accomplishment, are ways in which the stirrings of our true identity have been recognized. Little do we realize

**Making changes can seem like a lot of work,
especially when the burden has been heavy.**

We can start making changes by taking baby steps.

changes in our inner makeup or the use we have made of our power to think.

To go beyond this habitual cycle, we must make a decision that we want life to be different and that we are willing to do things differently. This is why we profit so highly by setting aside time to go beyond mind into an awareness that includes our higher self, the Source of our being. By stilling the mind, we open up to the feeling of being connected to Source. The greater the awareness of this connection, the more we will come to know our true self. We call this space of awareness being centered. We call the activity, Spiritual Practice.

Daily Spiritual Practice builds our consciousness of oneness, oneness with Source, oneness with our true self, and eventually a feeling of oneness with all of life. We begin to see changes happening in our lives as we allow Source to bring new ideas and patterns of behavior into play. Changes don't always come quickly. It takes conscious effort to lead our thoughts and emotional responses towards healthy, happy living. The rewards are self gratifying, however, and when they begin to come, they reinforce our commitment to continue our Spiritual Practices.

Breathing techniques are one form of Spiritual Practice, but there are many ways in which we demonstrate our understanding that we are one with Source. Affirmative Prayer, Positive Affirmations, Journaling and Creative Visualization are some of the Spiritual Practices that support our journey into greater happiness. There are many books written on each of these topics. Our growth depends on our willingness to explore new ideas and put them into practice when inspired to do so.

Chapter 3

Appreciation of Self

*The most terrifying thing is to accept oneself
completely.*
Carl Jung

Spiritual Practices bring on a kind of anointing or blessing. No longer do we need to think or feel like we are victims of the world around us. We are developing skills and practicing techniques that work with our authentic power, the kind of power that comes from being in touch with our true identity, Source. We are Spirit. We are more than flesh and bones and we are more than our history. As we receive the inspiration of Spirit, our thoughts become elevated. We see how things fit together, how everything is connected. We expand our point of view and grow in our ability to accept others as they are. We learn to trust our own process of awakening to a more peaceful, productive, joyful way of living. Because we see our own growth, we can share confidence that others may also make changes for the better in their lives. Our need to judge begins to fall away and in its place our hearts open to compassion. We find that the Spiritual Practice of forgiveness takes on new meaning. We willingly allow ourselves to be healed by the Spirit of love that lives within us.

The fuel that feeds the fire of Spirit is appreciation. The fire of Spirit is inspiration from Source. On our way to true happiness, we cannot underestimate the value of appreciation. We are always with ourselves. The thoughts we have about ourselves determine the kind of experiences we will have in life. We will rise in consciousness when we recognize our good qualities and

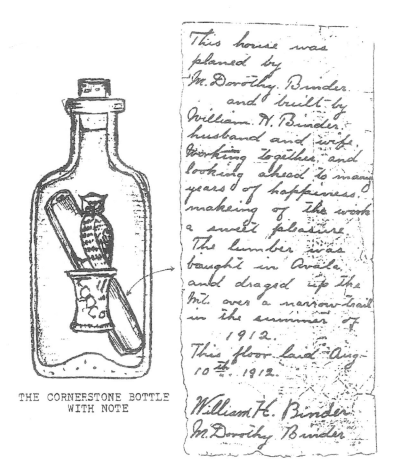

THE CORNERSTONE BOTTLE
WITH NOTE

When we appreciate the opportunity to make changes in our lives, we are in tune with a sweetness that holds out hope that our future will be filled with greater good and satisfaction.
The work becomes "sweet pleasure."

praise them. When we praise something, we lift it up. We are not trying to be better than anyone else; we are noticing that a particular quality of Source is being demonstrated. These qualities of Source, beauty, truth, wisdom, wholeness, love, abundance, balance, peace, and power are in everyone. Most of us deny our own truth by finding fault and concentrating on what is wrong with us. Could we but pause to find a tiny expression of one of these qualities, we would begin to express more of it. This is what appreciation and praise accomplish.

It may be scary to begin this process. We may think we'll become too self centered and selfish. We might even feel embarrassed. Have we ever been in a situation where a compliment was given and watched the recipient deny or discount what has been said? Underneath our outer shell of confidence or boisterous behaviors there lurks an idea that we aren't worthy. Stepping into appreciation of self may be a huge leap for some of us. We might consider asking others what they appreciate about us if we are having trouble getting started.

Let's consider the basics. Are we appreciating our health, our ability to see the world around us, the freedom to move about? Can we hear or sing or play an instrument? Do we know how to use a cell phone, a computer, a DVD player, or digital camera? Are we thoughtful and share from our store of abundance? Are we called to volunteer at a non-profit organization?

What about the positive changes we have already made in our lives? Have we spoken a kind word at just the right time? Appreciating ourselves opens our hearts to love. This helps us to know the Source is with us. To know the Source is with us is a pathway to true happiness.

There must have been quite a feeling of accomplishment
for this couple as the homestead took shape and their son
grew up. Imagine being out in the wilderness and
celebrating by getting all dressed up for Sunday dinner.
Matilda was a lady with flair!

Pets were important, not only as companions, but they were helpful in keeping down the mouse and gopher population. Were they also baby sitters?

Living five miles from town and three miles from your nearest neighbor made appreciation of others even more meaningful. Sharing a meal was a treat as Matilda was a great cook. Chicken was a favorite dinner.

Chapter 4

Appreciation of Others

*Appreciation is a wonderful thing. It makes what is excellent
in others belong to us as well.*
Voltaire

How can we underestimate the value of our family
and friends in their role of contributing to our happiness?
Our relationship with these particular people shapes our
experiences and helps form our beliefs from infancy. Our
parents may have fallen short of our expectations, but in
the gap, we have been given the opportunity to choose
again in our own lives. We can take the good and expand
on it or reverse the bad by correcting it as we interact with
others. Life is in our minds; our thoughts and feelings determine the quality of our experiences. Forgiveness plays
an important role in healing any differences we may have
had with our parents, friends and teachers. It is a gift to
ourselves when we let the past go. The higher vibration of
appreciation brings greater happiness than criticism, con-
demnation, victim thinking, and holding on to grudges.
To consciously seek out the good in others can become a
game that rivals winning the lottery in feelings of goodness, happiness and peace. Are we willing to begin?

Where do we want to bring about positive changes
in our relationships? Is our child having difficulty in
school? Have we sincerely looked for places to praise his
efforts? Or do we complain about his poor study habits
and ineffective teachers? Do we avoid certain people because of their race, religion, political leanings or financial
standing? These feelings of separation are keeping us
away from the flow of Spirit. It is surprising what kind of

shift we may experience if we would be willing to look for something to appreciate in all people.

Appreciating others can become a game. Can we catch someone being kind to an elderly person? Can we notice the detailed attention a co worker has given to bringing forth a new product or service? Is the food especially tasty, and are we quick to give a compliment? Have we witnessed a young mother dealing with her child in a responsible manner? Has someone let us into traffic on a busy afternoon, and did we wave a friendly, "Thank You?"

Every day we are the beneficiaries of the services of others. Our connection and dependency on each other is quite amazing. There are exceptions, but they rarely exist. Countless individuals are responsible for providing the food we eat, the clothes we wear, the companies we work for, and the equipment we use to carry on our daily activities. We take for granted most of what comes to us, even if we live at a poverty level.

The law of increase works through the expression of gratitude and appreciation. We can bring about positive changes simply by noticing what is working and silently or audibly expressing our appreciation. We all thrive on positive reinforcement, but we seem to be wired for pointing out what is not working. There is an unwritten code, especially in the restaurant industry, that good service is rewarded by leaving a tip beyond the cost of the meal. This is one way of showing appreciation. If the server has been attentive and joyful, the tip may be larger, indicating a greater appreciation of the server's efforts. In turn, the server will be motivated to continue his or her thoughtful attention to the next customer. What we pay attention to, we cause to increase.

Happiness starts from within. The more we notice the good things that are going on, the greater our feeling of connection. There's always another way of seeing a person or situation. By setting our intention on finding the good, we will begin to hear our higher thoughts. From Spirit, we get insight and a shift of perception. As we watch this begin to happen within our

consciousness, we experience the joy of personal transformation. Appreciating others is a powerful Spiritual
Practice.

It's a wonder to behold the creativity and abundance
that Matilda and William created in the wilderness.
Matilda enjoyed being a stylish lady even there.

Chapter 5

Appreciation of Abundance

*When you are grateful fear disappears
and abundance appears.*
Anthony Robbins

Fear has gripped the hearts of almost everyone around the subject of money. Our relationship with money can give us insight into our level of trust in our Source. Past conditioning has erroneously led us to build a scarcity consciousness. We may have come to believe that there is never enough. Consequently, we continue to experience a life of living on the edge of financial disaster. We may hoard material objects in preparation for this expected disaster; or we might accumulate enormous debt with credit cards in an attempt to prove that we are worthy of "having it all." These dysfunctions around money are reflections of a lack of understanding about our Source and the laws of abundance.

The truth is, we are extensions of Source, not separated entities. What is the nature of Source? We can look to the natural world to answer this question. By studying even one plant, we can begin to appreciate the intelligence needed to create it. Within the plant there must be harmony, order, balance, beauty, power, wholeness. Source has provided a way for this one plant to become many. Abundance is part of the plan. Why would we think Source had extended itself as us with fewer resources than a plant?

These are radishes grown on the homestead.
The soil must have been quite fertile.
Do you wonder how they ate them?

Our Spiritual inheritance has provided a means for us to be abundantly supplied with everything necessary for a successful, happy life.

We work with this truth by studying life at a deeper level. What are the laws of abundance? Circulation is a primary law with which we must cooperate consciously, if we are to move from scarcity thinking to abundant living. We see this principle at work as we watch the cycles of life. Life flows into expression. Water from the lake evaporates in the sunshine, accumulates again as clouds, spills itself as rain and replenishes the supply of water in the lake. Circulation is movement. By cooperating with this law, we increase our supply of abundance.

The Law of Circulation and the Law of Focus of Attention go together. We may be so focused on what we don't have, that we overlook the good that is already ours. Our feelings of lack overshadow our feelings of plenty. What we pay attention to, we increase! Here is a clue for transformation. We can start by appreciating the abundance that we have and also the abundance that we see in the world of appearances. It is up to us to choose the direction of our growth. Isn't it more fun to find places that we see abundance expressing than to dwell on lack? As we start circulating thoughts of abundance by focusing our attention on the good, we feel different. We activate the Law of Mind Action which returns to us in like manner. Happy thoughts bring more happiness—and more abundance of good.

It's almost impossible to estimate the number of thoughts we have in a day. What kind of thoughts are they? Our bodies have trillions of cells. Could we count the hairs on our heads? How many needles does that fir tree have? How much food does a fast food chain need to buy in a single day? How many stars are there in the northern hemisphere? By giving our attention to the abundance around us, we are transforming our basic idea of Source. We are aligning ourselves with truth. Our Source is not lacking, has already provided the means for the continuation of abundance and will appear in our own

23

This strawberry field was all plowed by hand with the help of a horse and mule. Apparently the climate was perfect for this crop.

There was an abundance of plant life from which to create hanging baskets and vines to shelter the pergola
area from summer sunshine.

lives as we get into harmony with truth. It is entirely possible to change our thoughts and feelings about our own abundance and move into new levels of expression. A happy person feels happy because he or she knows that Source is providing the good that is desired. We remember what we pay attention to, increases.

There are other actions that reinforce our understanding of the laws of abundance and circulation. Being aware of Source's generosity, we begin to duplicate this tendency in our own lives. We can look for ways to share our good. We can allow love to inspire us to help others. We can give our time to causes that make our world a better place in which to live. We can circulate our financial wealth to institutions and organizations that encourage self empowerment. The more we give without strings attached, the more we build our faith in the law of circulation. This is the law of increased abundance.

We may also need to evaluate our ability to receive. The law of circulation and generosity implies that there are givers and receivers. Old beliefs and patterns of behavior may stop the flow of abundance if we are unwilling to let ourselves be blessed. We are part of the whole. Our acceptance of generosity means that someone else has the full joy of giving. It is fun to receive a thank you card or a bouquet of flowers from a neighbor's garden. Let's be gracious receivers as well as givers. Acceptance is another way of showing appreciation.

Chapter 6

Appreciation of Beauty

Life is full of beauty. Notice it.
Notice the bumble bee, the small child, and the smiling faces. Smell
the rain, and feel the wind.
Live your life to the fullest potential...
Ashley Smith

The Source is powerfully felt in the presence of beauty. Something within us stops for a few moments to take a deep breath and experience our oneness. Our hearts long for connection and beauty brings us to this kind of deep satisfaction. We gaze at mountain streams, hike tall peaks, visit beautiful parks, create garden sanctuaries around our homes, and decorate our tables with fresh flowers.

Beauty means different things to different people. We see homes, commercial buildings, cars and numerous other products beautifully designed to attract our attention. Our individual tastes determine our acceptance of what is beautiful. The ability to create beauty in our experience of life comes from our Source. There is a longing to express the unlimited reservoir of beauty within us. A child takes a crayon to draw. The artist labors with his oils to put down on canvas the experience of beauty he feels in his soul. The dress designer listens for ideas from Spirit and produces a whole new fashion trend. A homemaker moves furniture around, again, searching for the perfect way to express greater beauty. We have an inner yearning to express ourselves.

Music is created to stimulate an experience of the soul. When the sounds we hear strike the cord of beauty within us, we are uplifted. This is the ultimate gift of beauty; it temporarily removes our attention from the discords of the world and puts us back in harmony with the symphony of heaven on earth. The urge to be at harmony with life causes us to seek out all kinds of temporary means to accomplish the goal. The ancients sought out ways to decorate their basic utensils such as pottery jars and woven baskets. Our clothing, our jewelry our streamlined cars, our endless array of household items used for decoration, are all ways that we answer the call of satisfying our need for beauty.

Through consciously looking for beauty, we are focusing our attention on what's right and true with the world. It is easy to complain, but in the state of appreciation, our consciousness is being prepared for inspiration from on high. We give wings to our thoughts and the wind of Spirit gives new direction to our tasks. We see things from a different perspective; we go beyond our usual ways of responding.

What we focus on is a decision. To fully realize our greatest potential, we must become the masters of our thoughts and feelings. Appreciation opens the door to our magnificence because it opens our souls to the love of our Creator. Our Creator is our cheer leader and Source of the good that flows through us into the world.

Happiness depends on our awareness of this presence. Appreciation is such an easy way to reconnect with peace and joy. Let's take time out to watch a colorful sunset, stroll through a flower shop, or picnic beside a tree lined stream in a grassy meadow.

William and son are resting under the pergola enjoying
the fruits of his labor. Each limb of the cover, gate and
fence were all cut by hand and nailed together.

What an accomplishment to have made such an orderly
display of flowers, steps, deck, banister and path. Love
can do it all!

Chapter 7

Appreciation of Order

Those who lead disciplined and orderly lifestyles.... achieve all their goals and progress.
Yajur Veda quotes

It has been said that order is the first rule of Heaven. In our imagination, we would surely agree that heaven on earth would include a sense of peace about everything that concerns us. To have peace would mean that consistency exists; that one can count on certain things to happen in an orderly and timely fashion. The opposite of order is confusion and chaos. When we live in this state of affairs, we create undue stress in our lives. We seem to be under the constant threat of impending disaster. Our happiness is only a fragile hope.

What seems orderly to me may not reflect another person's sense of order. It is a feeling about the flow of life. If we are feeling lost, overwhelmed by circumstances, depressed, angry, and critical about the way things are going, it is time to investigate our habits, attitudes and behaviors. We can change these aspects of ourselves and choose a new path to travel. We may want to seek out professional counseling. We might simply begin with an assessment of the way we take care of our basic needs such as eating right and getting enough rest. Do we take care of the things we have and use? Do we keep our word and carry through our commitments? Are we balancing our work, play, education and recreation?

It takes courage to look squarely into the face of our habits and make a decision to change. The rewards, however, are clearly evidenced by the new sense of freedom, peace and happiness we feel. A small change, and the accompanying results, become fuel to tackle the next change as we check off the items on our list for self improvement. No one else can create order for us that is lasting. We have to want to maintain the change through our own choice. We have to see the value ourselves.

We can clean out a closet, reorganize our garage, and circulate unused clothing and household items. We can choose a bed time that allows for enough rest to work and play at our full capacity. We can bring our eating habits into alignment with health principles that build strong bodies. We can set up routines, write them down and celebrate our progress as we go along. All of these activities send a message to our subconscious mind, a message that says we are ready to experience a new sense of order in our lives.

It would be an interesting experiment to become conscious of how order looks in the commercial world. When a business is not operating under the laws of order, it soon fails. What can we appreciate about the way a successful business operates? Are the products arranged in an appealing way? Are there people available to answer our questions? Do they stand behind their products with a return policy? Do they conduct sales in a timely manner which appeals to the needs of the changing seasons?

Perhaps we can duplicate these qualities in our own lives. We can evaluate the appearance of our living space and simplify or make changes accordingly. We can look for ways to handle our finances more effectively. We can balance our activities as seasons change in order to enjoy the benefits of variety. We can show respect and understanding for the people around us. We can remember to nourish our family members with time and attention. We can create intentions and goals together when appropriate. Every successful business plan includes these elements.

By starting with the end in mind, we focus the creative power that lives within us. Our goals and intentions establish our purpose and allow for an orderly flow of activities that all point in one direction. Our feelings of order are magnified when we know where we want to go. When we frequently remind ourselves of our greater purpose, we are less likely to be distracted by non essentials. The order within our thinking has taken root and we stay focused on what we really want, not what we want in the moment. True happiness comes by feeling empowered from within.

One must appreciate the wisdom it would take to capture
a swarm of bees. The strawberries and other plants benefited from their work.

Chapter 8

Appreciation of Wisdom

Be happy. It's one way of being wise.
Sidonie Gabrielle

The Source of true wisdom is within us. Our usual method for seeking wisdom is to use our past experience as a reference point. Next, we search outside ourselves for someone else's ideas. We can gain insight through these avenues of exploration, but where is the true wisdom we are seeking? Does it come from our ability to align this information and make it useful for our particular situation? Even this cannot be called true wisdom. When true wisdom is revealed, it comes as a feeling of knowing. We cannot be talked out of this kind of authentic wisdom. We call it intuition or our sixth sense.

Intuition is a gift given to everyone, but our ability to draw on it takes concentration and willingness. Our five senses give impressions of the world around us. They can remind us of previous experiences, and before we know it, we have made judgments that may be totally irrelevant to the present moment. We repeat old behaviors and remain stuck in the past. To move forward, we must go deeper to find the appropriate meaning for a current situation.

Our happiness depends on our ability to let the past be transformed by the voice of intuition. Intuition's voice, or the voice for Truth, Source or Spirit, within us, is soft and is easily missed. It could come in words, but it might just be a deep feeling or what we referred to above as unshakable knowing. Our human personality also has a voice; what it tells us is often based on fear and the idea of separation. Its thought system is self centered and never based on the principle of oneness and love. Its voice is loud and usually the first voice we hear. If we want to experience consistent happiness in our lives, we must learn to distinguish between the two voices within us. Next, we must be willing to follow intuition's guidance.

As we live from intuition, we begin to see authentic wisdom shaping our decisions. We notice that life becomes less confusing, that we are experiencing a greater sense of order. Our responses to people around us soften. Before, our reactions brought us conflict and anger. Now we listen to the voice that shows us how to see things from love's perspective. We can truly appreciate the changes brought about by our ability to consciously live our lives from true wisdom.

When we find ourselves in the middle of a difficult situation, it may seem almost impossible to find that quiet, reassuring voice of wisdom. We need Spiritual Practices or mental techniques that quiet our minds and soothe our emotions. We may want to investigate several methods of meditation until we find one that works best for us. Meditation helps us go beyond our mental noise to a feeling of deep union, peace and stillness.

One such technique is especially helpful in making decisions. Sitting comfortably in a quiet space, we begin by remembering times in which love has been deeply felt. We concentrate on these experiences for about ten minutes. Then we free the mind from these memories by focusing our attention on the feelings of love in our hearts. As we focus, the feelings grow stronger. Now we are ready to ask for direction about our concern. This time, we listen from our hearts, not our heads. We are going beyond our usual thinking mind to the Source of wisdom. We might question the answer we get. If so, we can sit with it for a day or two and see what happens. Let's see what thoughts and feelings come up. This technique can be effective in reaching that place of knowing. It is just as important to know what we do not want, as it is to know what we do want.

By developing our ability to commune with the Source of wisdom within, we grow in self confidence. We

36

are never alone or separated from the Source of our good. We have a divine companion that accompanies us everywhere, one whose only job is to insure our happiness. Every positive thought is an opportunity for gratitude. Every shift of perception to truth is a chance to appreciate the One who goes with us. Every narrow escape on the freeway is evidence of the Source's protection. Let us strengthen our habit of gratitude and appreciation. We, who see blessings, see the wisdom of Source at work. The more we see wisdom, the greater will be our own experience of blessings. The law of increase continues to work on our behalf by increasing our experience of happiness.

This is no ordinary gate! William put in a lot
of time and effort in creating this entrance to Oak Terrace,
as the homestead was called.

Chapter 9

Appreciation of Creativity

Creativity is inventing, experimenting, growing,
taking risks, breaking rules, making mistakes,
and having fun.
Mary Lou Cook

Life springs into form and experience through our creativity. Nothing can contribute more to our happiness and joy than to have a realization of this magnificent gift. We powerfully duplicate the nature of Source through our desire to create. It's as though we have an inner compass pointing to self expression. We may think of it as creativity, but actually, we are extending the power, imagination, substance, intelligence, and generosity of Source within us. We use what has already been given and extend it outward.

Inspiration for anything new begins with a hidden motivation to bring more good (Source), into our lives. We know the presence of Source by many names; beauty, oneness, love, abundance, joy, wholeness, freedom, wisdom, balance, and peace. These facets live in the invisible world of Spirit as our inheritance. We may want to paint our house a different color; deeper within, is our desire to enjoy more beauty. We may be searching for a life partner; deeper within is the desire to feel our oneness with Source. We hunger for a better paying job; deeper within is the desire to experience the unlimited abundance of Spirit or Source.

What we refer to as creativity is really Source expressing itself through us in ways unique to us. Spirit flows through every aspect of our beings; our mental

Matilda created this dress on a treadle sewing machine.
She was an artist, a photographer and superb seamstress.

being, our physical being, and our emotional being. Inventions are the result of a kind of mindset with a specific purpose to fulfill. We refer to this part of our being as the problem-solver. It is our capacity to choose and make decisions.

We have free will. As we utilize this capacity to choose, we begin to discover that we can make choices that do not duplicate the nature of Source. When we do so, however, we find that we are not experiencing love, joy and peace.

We may have inherited the capacity for wisdom, but we don't necessarily know how to access it. Our habitual responses to the world and our past experiences may have led to a belief system built on fear and separation and with that belief system comes an inner voice filled with fear and worry As we listen to this voice, we misuse our power to create.

Another voice is available, but it takes training and willingness to be still and listen. The wisdom from this voice is centered in love and good will for everyone. When we stay tuned to this voice, we draw a sense of satisfaction as we survey our accomplishments. Our hearts are filled with appreciation; we have accessed the deeper happiness within.

The capacity to create is enormous. We can appreciate this unlimited power that lies within us by viewing our immediate surroundings.

The 20th Century witnessed more changes for the human species than any other time in history. These all came into being through the well spring of inspiration and creativity.

What do we want to bring into our lives? Our clarity about our desires draws ideas, feelings, energy, knowledge, people and situations to us. We have stirred the pot and its coming to a boil. People call this the Law of Attraction. We are free at any moment to create a whole new life for ourselves.

Our true happiness lies in our willingness to let the past go, to forgive ourselves and others for past mistakes and to have the courage to examine old beliefs that no long serve us. This calls for increased awareness. What are we thinking and feeling? We want to ask these questions because the creative aspect of our mind works by moving into action based on how we focus our attention.

We may be entertaining new thoughts, but our deeper feelings are fearful of change. The deeper mind of creation operates on our beliefs. Beliefs are filled with feeling and negative feelings sabotage our desire for change. As we become aware of these false beliefs and face them with truth, we free ourselves from limitation. This is Spiritual Practice. It is the way we return to the joy and happiness that was intended for us in the beginning.

By choosing to work consciously with the laws of creativity, we come to appreciate just how wonderful life can be. We are no longer victims. We take our power back and become part of the solution. The voice for love now has a clear channel to express Itself through us. We awaken refreshed for the day, certain that good things are ready to unfold. We have confidence that the voice of wisdom and love is guiding our thoughts and actions towards a higher purpose. The genie within us is about to shine wonderful surprises into our lives.

Chapter 10

Appreciation of Holiness

Holiness is happiness;
and the more you have of the former,
the more you will undoubtedly enjoy of the latter.
John Angell James

Lasting happiness can only come to us as we recognize and accept our own holiness. Until then, we find ourselves engaging in an endless search for an illusive feeling that disappears just as we draw near. We look for our soul mate and an income that provides us with the ability to buy all the "stuff" we think we need, Maybe another college degree would do it or the newest health fad would erase the years of physical neglect and give us the feeling we want. We get high on drugs, go to the mall, disappear at the keyboard or plant another geranium; surely the answer is there. Ironically, we are blinded by the temptations that lead us away from peace, the peace and happiness that are our birthright. We don't see the connection between our nagging dissatisfaction and our lack of Spiritual attention.

There are countless religions; each one has in some way been pointing to the sacredness of life and the One who has given us that life. Religions are systems organized around beliefs about how it all happened and how we might best express the gift. Each has its own standards and theories. Many have arisen from one person who experienced a deeper connection to Source. Because of the experience, greater wisdom began to flow from his or her presence. Interested others gathered around to learn how they might also find the same connection and greater wisdom. Rules, ceremonies, and a hierarchy of leadership began to unfold. Over the years, much of the original sacredness and meaning have gotten lost. We may have become suspicious of organized religion and turned completely away from it. In doing so, we might have overlooked the importance of Spiritual communion right within our own life temple.

We are Spiritual beings and have been designed to experience our sacredness at will. Spiritual Practices, such as meditation, help us come to know our real selves. We feel our own holiness as we still our minds and surrender into the love that created us. Once we get a taste of this oneness, we find ourselves looking at life differently. Big changes don't always happen right away, but we can sense a shift. We begin to appreciate life. Our tendency to harshly judge others diminishes. We return to the still small voice of love for guidance instead of the appearances of the world. Our times of quiet reflection and appreciation open our hearts and minds to inspiration. Our understanding increases. We see our dysfunctional patterns of behavior and get help in releasing them. We practice self forgiveness which translates into forgiveness for all. We stop seeking our good and are more interested in revealing the presence of Source. We ask, "How can I bring more beauty, love, joy, peace, wisdom, abundance, order, and harmony into the world?"

As we move to higher consciousness, we learn to have compassion for ourselves and others. Punishment is a man made idea. Spirit works through natural consequences; we see the contrast and move towards the goal we truly want. It becomes and inner journey to enlightenment. We feed and encourage ourselves as we recognize our successes. We rejoice in our little steps of progress, and what we focus on increases

Everything is holy when we look through the eyes of Spirit. Truth has its own light and those who are advanced in Spiritual awareness look for the truth beyond the man-made world of appearances. All beings are holy;

As Christmas was celebrated, William and Matilda must have paused to give thanks for the many blessings they had experienced in fulfilling their dreams of having their own land. Little Morton received a Teddy bear from a family friend who lived far away. It would have taken a whole day to go into town five miles away in order to get the package. No UPS in those days!

we come from the same Source. Most of us live in ignorance of the beauty that lies within, but that doesn't mean it isn't there. We are learning to identify ourselves with truth. Can we remind ourselves of our holiness throughout each day? Spirit's eyes can just as easily be our eyes and ears when we set our intention in this direction.

The eyes of Spirit are soft, overlooking everything that does not reflect our Source. Spirit is the connection or bridge between our humanness and our true Self. It has the ability to translate everything into holiness. How blessed we are to have within us this memory of Source. Our experience of life can hold so much more when we make the shift to asking for Spirit's wisdom. As we become consistent in this Spiritual practice, we find our souls becoming peaceful and satisfied. No longer do we feel alone. We feel our wholeness and trust that all is working together for a greater purpose. We become the open channels through which the light of truth shines on a forgiven world.

The dream come true:
Oak Terrace after seven years.

Chapter 11

Putting It All Together

*The miracle, or the power, that elevates the few
is to be found in their industry, application,
and perseverance under the prompting of a brave,
determined spirit.*
Mark Twain

We are holy beings. Our potential for loving life and living love is endless. Appreciation of Source with Its many facets is the key to happiness. We may use other names for Source; God, Creator, Father, Spirit, Presence, or Love. Whatever name we choose, however, must invoke a feeling of deep connection and goodness. We may also have different names for the way in which Source communicates directly; Holy Spirit, Voice for Love, Intuition, Still Small Voice. Again, we choose the name that resonates with a feeling of connection to the All Mighty.

By now, we are familiar with the concept that true happiness does not depend on getting things in the world. We are already whole. Spiritually, we already have everything needed to experience happiness. We have guidance and the means to bring new experiences into our lives through our focus of attention. Our true calling is to express the qualities of Source each and every moment of our lives. Our happiness depends on it.

Daily Spiritual Practice brings us back to center and the memory of our true inheritance. A cheerful attitude arises as we remember that we are Spiritual beings. This is a temporary home and becomes a delightful place when we align ourselves with truth. Appreciation is the golden key to experiencing heaven on earth. As awakened Spiritual beings, we have an important part to play in the transformation of consciousness. We show the world around us greater possibilities by being the light we were created to shine.

We carry the light through appreciation! When we acknowledge or appreciate the light we see in others, we are seeing a reflection of Source. As we speak our words of appreciation, we fan the flame of Spirit. Praise and gratitude are food for our souls. Let us find ways to look through negativity and remember that Source is present everywhere. What is not love is a call for love. We are God beings, holy, magnificent and infinitely creative. Let us come to love and appreciate ourselves deeply. Let us speak appreciation and gratitude to others as never before. In this Holy instant, **now**, we can choose to make a difference in someone's life.

Who can tell where the fallout will change a life forever? Perhaps it will be our own life, as we finally discover the Source of True Happiness. Let us shine!

Chapter 12

Appreciation: A Prayer for Life

*Appreciation is the highest form of prayer,
for it acknowledges the presence of good
wherever you shine the light
of your thankful thoughts.*
Alan Cohen

To be fully present in appreciation is to offer an affirmative prayer. Affirmative prayers are the opposite of a prayer of petition. They recognize that there is no separation between Source and ourselves, so they simply affirm a particular goodness that is already available to us. There are usually five components that make up this type of prayer.

They begin with a **Recognition** of Source. When we show our appreciation for something, we are identifying Source. We may see this expressed as Joy, Love, Peace, Abundance, Wholeness, Balance, Wisdom, Creativity, Health and Order to name a few of the qualities of Source.

The second step is **Unification** with Source. Since we are appreciating a quality of Source, we are already joined in consciousness by becoming aware of it.

Thirdly, by focusing our attention on a quality of Source through appreciation, we are singling out the kind of good that we want more of. We are having a **Realization**, the third component. This happens as a feeling and a thought that sets in motion a series of events that will bring us more of the kind of good that we appreciated. We can call this process the Law of Mind Action.

It feels good when we appreciate anything. This opens our hearts to the experience of **Gratitude**, the fourth component of our affirmative prayer.

Fifth, as we rest in gratitude, we become peaceful and have a sense of well being or happiness. Secure in our relationship with Source, through appreciation, we just naturally **Release** our prayer and know that all is well with even greater good on its way.

In summary, appreciation generates a natural affirmative prayer as it embraces the five ingredients of Recognition, Unification, Realization, Gratitude and Release. To appreciate is to pray!

The following is an example of how to use the idea of Affirmative Prayer. We start by identifying a quality of Source and build our prayer around it. Here is a prayer built around the quality of Health:

Recognition:

I appreciate the vibrant expression of energy that I see as hundreds of people go to work, attend to the business of life, and engage in all kinds of wonderful activities. This energy comes from Source.

Unification:

As I focus on all this vitality, I know that   I, too, am a part of this greater plan of life. I praise my awareness and appreciation of this life force at work in me as well.

Realization:

Through my awareness of Source as Health, I begin to notice how many activities of my body are taken care of without my conscious effort. The food I eat is digested properly, assimilated, circulated and eliminated according to divine intelligence.

I cooperate with the laws of health by keeping my mind free of worry and appreciating the freedom I already experience as I go about my daily routine.

I forgive myself and others as a way of keeping my emotional nature clear of disturbances. The Spiritual design of my physical expression is free to express its wholeness right now.

Gratitude:

As I appreciate my blessings, my heart opens in gratitude for the health I already show forth and for the increased vitality and healing that is on its way. Thank you Source!

Release:

I am now aware of a peaceful feeling and confidently release my Prayer of Appreciation into the Law of Mind Action expecting to be healed.

And so it is. Amen.

Expect Miracles! By aligning our minds with the energy of appreciation, we are calling our good to us in miraculous ways. If doubt enters, we can remind ourselves that Source's will for us is perfect happiness. When we stay positive, we will see wonderful things unfold. We keep our faith strong by giving thanks for the good that is already in our lives.

About the Author

Rev. Frances Lancaster is an independent minister lecturing, teaching, writing, and facilitating study groups. She has a degree in education from Washington State University and has written curriculum for both adults and children to use in Metaphysical churches. Rev. Frances has served in a leadership capacity in both local and international New Thought organizations. She lives in Hillsboro, Oregon where her passion centers on helping people learn to create fulfilling and productive lives as they serve one another through conscious connection with our Creator's inspiration and guidance.

WiseWoman Press

Books by Frances B. Lancaster

- *Abundance Now*
- *The 13th Commandment*
- *A Miracle of Love*

Books by Emma Curtis Hopkins

- *Resume*
- *The Gospel Series*
- *Class Lessons of 1888*
- *Self Treatments including Radiant I Am*
- *High Mysticism*
- *Genesis Series 1894*
- *Esoteric Philosophy in Spiritual Science*
- *Drops of Gold Journal*
- *Judgment Series*
- *Bible Interpretations: Series I, thru XVII*

Books by Ruth L. Miller

- *Unveiling Your Hidden Power: Emma Curtis Hopkins' Metaphysics for the 21st Century*
- *Coming into Freedom: Emily Cady's Lessons in Truth for the 21st Century*
- *150 Years of Healing: The Founders and Science of New Thought*
- *Power Beyond Magic: Ernest Holmes Biography*
- *Power to Heal: Emma Curtis Hopkins Biography*
- *The Power of Unity: Charles Fillmore Biography*
- *Power of Thought: Phineas P. Quimby Biography*
- *The Power of Insight: Thomas Troward Biography*
- *The Power of the Self: Ralph Waldo Emerson Biography*
- *Uncommon Prayer*
- *Spiritual Success*
- *Finding the Path*

www.wisewomanpress.com

CPSIA information can be obtained at www.ICGtesting.com
Printed in the USA
BVOW07s0822081013

333189BV00008B/168/P